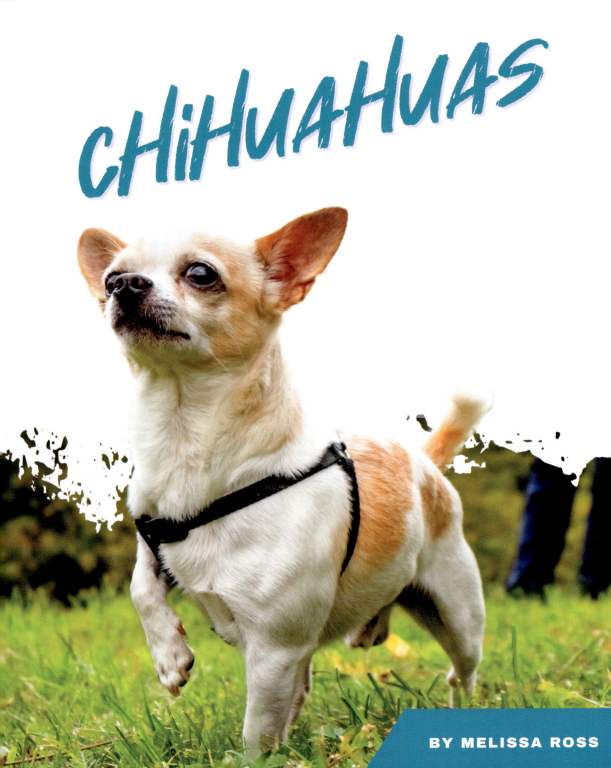

DOG BREEDS

CHIHUAHUAS

BY MELISSA ROSS

WWW.APEXEDITIONS.COM

Copyright © 2025 by Apex Editions, Mendota Heights, MN 55120. All rights reserved. No part of this book may be reproduced or utilized in any form or by any means without written permission from the publisher.

Apex is distributed by North Star Editions:
sales@northstareditions.com | 888-417-0195

Produced for Apex by Red Line Editorial.

Photographs ©: iStockphoto, cover, 19, 20–21, 22–23; Shutterstock Images, 1, 4–5, 6, 7, 8–9, 15, 16–17, 18, 24–25, 26, 27, 29; Florilegius/Alamy, 10–11; Ida Pap/Alamy, 13; Keystone Pictures USA/Keystone Press/Alamy, 14

Library of Congress Control Number: 2023921617

ISBN
978-1-63738-905-8 (hardcover)
978-1-63738-945-4 (paperback)
979-8-89250-042-5 (ebook pdf)
979-8-89250-003-6 (hosted ebook)

Printed in the United States of America
Mankato, MN
082024

NOTE TO PARENTS AND EDUCATORS

Apex books are designed to build literacy skills in striving readers. Exciting, high-interest content attracts and holds readers' attention. The text is carefully leveled to allow students to achieve success quickly. Additional features, such as bolded glossary words for difficult terms, help build comprehension.

TABLE OF CONTENTS

CHAPTER 1
Tiny Traveler 4

CHAPTER 2
Chihuahua History 10

CHAPTER 3
Little Dogs 16

CHAPTER 4
Chihuahua Care 22

COMPREHENSION QUESTIONS • 28
GLOSSARY • 30
TO LEARN MORE • 31
ABOUT THE AUTHOR • 31
INDEX • 32

CHAPTER 1

Tiny Traveler

An owner scoops up his Chihuahua. He places her in a small carrier. The little dog is ready for another trip to the airport.

Dogs should stay in carriers when traveling by car or plane.

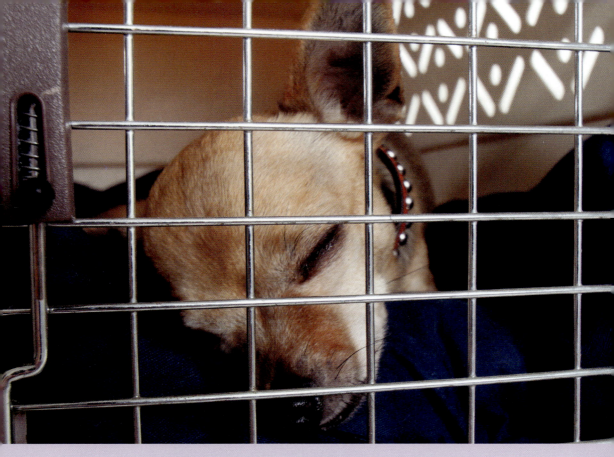

Owners can train their Chihuahuas to stay calm while traveling.

On the plane, the owner slides the carrier under the seat. The Chihuahua lies down inside it. She naps on a soft blanket.

STAYING WARM

Chihuahuas have small bodies and thin coats. They get cold easily. Cold or wet weather can make them sick. They may need blankets to stay warm.

Chihuahuas can wear jackets to stay warm on cold days.

Chihuahuas' small size makes them good travel dogs.

The plane lands a few hours later. The owner and Chihuahua take a taxi to their hotel. Their room is small. But it has plenty of space for the Chihuahua to run around.

FAST FACT

Chihuahuas are the smallest dogs in the world.

CHAPTER 2

Chihuahua History

Chihuahuas are related to an **ancient** dog called the Techichi. Techichis were small dogs. They lived in Mexico, Central America, and South America.

Chihuahua-like dogs have been shown in art for hundreds of years.

Many **Indigenous** peoples owned Techichis. The Toltecs were one example. The Aztecs were another. These peoples also crossed the dogs with other breeds.

GUIDE DOGS

The Aztecs ruled Mexico from 1300 to 1521. Their nobles owned Techichis. When nobles died, dogs were buried with them. People believed the dogs would guide them in the afterlife.

Aztec people still live in Mexico today. They are called the Nahua people.

Chihuahuas have been part of American dog shows since 1890.

In the 1800s, these dogs became known as Chihuahuas. People sold them to **tourists**. Some tourists brought the Chihuahuas back to the United States. The dogs became popular pets there.

FAST FACT

Chihuahua is a state in Mexico. That's where the small dogs were first sold.

Chihuahua is the largest state in Mexico. It shares a border with Texas and New Mexico.

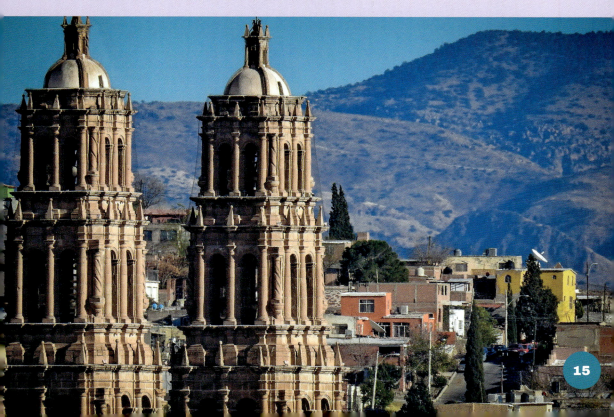

CHAPTER 3

Little Dogs

Chihuahuas are a toy breed. That means they are very small. Chihuahas stand 5 to 8 inches (13 to 20 cm) tall. They typically weigh up to 6 pounds (2.7 kg).

Toy breeds weigh less than 15 pounds (6.8 kg).

Many Chihuahuas have longer hair around their ears, neck, and legs.

Chihuahuas can have long or short fur. Their fur is typically brown, reddish, or cream colored. It may have spots, stripes, or patches of color.

FAST FACT

Some Chihuahuas have straight tails. Others have curved tails.

A Chihuahua's tail often curls back toward the dog's head.

Chihuahuas have round heads and short **muzzles**. They have large, round eyes. Their big ears are pointy and stand up.

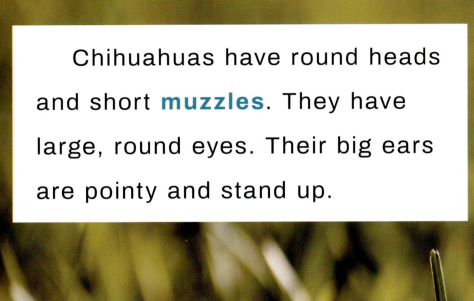

SUPER SMALL
Some Chihuahuas are especially tiny. They are called teacup Chihuahuas. They stand 6 inches (15 cm) high and weigh only 3 pounds (1.4 kg).

Chihuahuas are born with floppy ears. After a few months, their ears typically stand up.

CHAPTER 4

Chihuahua Care

Chihuahuas don't need much **grooming**. Long-haired Chihuahuas need weekly brushing. Dogs with short fur can be brushed less frequently. They also don't shed much.

Chihuahuas need baths once a month.

Owners can take Chihuahuas on short walks.

Chihuahuas make good dogs for apartments. They do well with small spaces. And they don't need much exercise. About 30 minutes to an hour each day is enough.

FAST FACT

Chihuahuas can get hurt easily because of their small size. Owners should be gentle.

Chihuahuas tend to be very close with just one person.

Chihuahuas are **loyal** to their owners. But they may bark at strangers. Training can help. Owners can work to **socialize** their dogs. That helps the dogs stay calm.

TIME FOR TRAINING

Chihuahuas are cute and little. So, some people don't think they need training. But that's not true. Poorly trained Chihuahuas may become **aggressive**.

Good training can help Chihuahuas get used to new people and other pets.

COMPREHENSION QUESTIONS

Write your answers on a separate piece of paper.

1. Write a few sentences explaining the main ideas of Chapter 2.

2. Would you like to own a Chihuahua? Why or why not?

3. Why do Chihuahuas do well in apartments?
   - A. Chihuahuas don't need lots of space.
   - B. Chihuahuas don't need exercise.
   - C. Chihuahuas need a lot of food.

4. Why would training help dogs be less aggressive?
   - A. Owners can teach dogs to bark louder.
   - B. Owners can teach dogs good ways to act.
   - C. Training helps dogs become more loyal.

5. What does **scoops** mean in this book?

An owner scoops up his Chihuahua. He places her in a small carrier.

   A. dresses
   B. lifts
   C. feeds

6. What does **frequently** mean in this book?

Long-haired Chihuahuas need weekly brushing. Dogs with short fur can be brushed less frequently.

   A. often
   B. gently
   C. quickly

Answer key on page 32.

GLOSSARY

aggressive
Strong and quick to attack.

ancient
Very old or from long ago.

grooming
The act of cleaning or caring for an animal's fur.

Indigenous
Related to the original people who lived in an area.

loyal
Loving and staying true to a person or thing.

muzzles
The jaws and noses of animals.

socialize
To introduce a dog to new people, places, and things.

tourists
People who visit a place for fun.

TO LEARN MORE

BOOKS

Frank, Sarah. *Chihuahuas*. Minneapolis: Lerner Publications, 2020.

Noll, Elizabeth. *Toy Dogs*. Minneapolis: Bellwether Media, 2021.

Pearson, Marie. *Dogs*. Mankato, MN: The Child's World, 2020.

ONLINE RESOURCES

Visit **www.apexeditions.com** to find links and resources related to this title.

ABOUT THE AUTHOR

Melissa Ross is the author of *Forensics for Kids* and other educational books for children. When she's not writing, she likes spending time with family, painting, and reading. She also enjoys walking her dog, who is quite a bit larger than a Chihuahua.

INDEX

A
ancient, 10
Aztecs, 12

C
Central America, 10

E
ears, 20
exercise, 25

F
fur, 18, 22

I
Indigenous, 12

M
Mexico, 10, 12, 15

S
small size, 4, 7, 9, 10, 15, 16, 20, 25
socializing, 26
South America, 10

T
teacup Chihuahuas, 20
Techichis, 10, 12
toy breed, 16
training, 26–27

ANSWER KEY:
1. Answers will vary; 2. Answers will vary; 3. A; 4. B; 5. B; 6. A